033497

Hill, Grace Livingston
    Life out of death/Grace Livingston Hill -
Mattituck, New York: Amereon House, 1983.
    97 p.

I.T.

Life Out Of Death

Life Out Of Death

by
Grace Livingston Hill

Amereon House

MATTITUCK

International Standard Book Number 0-89190-402-6

To order contact:
AMEREON HOUSE
the publishing division of
Amereon Ltd.
Box 1200
Mattituck, New York 11952

Manufactured in the United States of America by
The Mad Printers of Mattituck

033497

CONTENTS

INTRODUCTION

Grace Livingston Hill was born in Wellsville, New York April 16, 1865, the daughter of the Rev. Charles Montgomery Livingston and Marcia Macdonald Livingston. In her immediate family, there were seven Presbyterian ministers and even her name, Grace, was given her because of its theological meaning. Her mother wrote stories for religious magazines, and her aunt, Isabella Alden ("Pansy") was a writer of books for juveniles.

Grace was educated at home under private tutors and at the Cincinnati Art School and Elmira College, where she also studied art.

From childhood, Mrs. Hill had loved to write stories and as long as she lived, her mother was her helpful critic. Her aunt, Pansy, had her first story, *The Esselstynes*, published as a surprise when Grace was twelve.

In 1892, Grace Livingston married another Presbyterian minister, the Rev. Thomas Franklin Hill, and they had two daughters, Ruth and Margaret. He died in 1899, and her father immediately thereafter. Now Mrs. Hill was *obliged* to write to support her children. She conducted a weekly syndicated column in the religious papers, and she continued to write the novels which had begun as a hobby. Of her early days as a writer she said, "The truth is I never did consciously prepare for my literary career, and, furthermore, I have no method at all. Coming from a family of authors, it never came into my mind that preparation was necessary."

She was a tactile, prolific writer, turning out about three books a year. She wrote in the midst of interruptions, without disturbance. For an impressive total of more than 100 books and stories.

A widow for many years, in 1916 Mrs. Hill became Mrs. Flavius J. Lutz. Although she was always reluctant to discuss her second marriage, it was apparently not happy and led eventually to separation — Mrs. Hill was, of course, adamantly opposed to divorce. She lived in Swarthmore, Pennsylvania, in an old stone house, and worked in a second-story room "littered with books and magazines." Until her death at age 82 in 1947, she was active in church work, and spoke frequently before religious groups, traveling to her lecture engagements in a big automobile which she called her only luxury. She refused to charge anything for speaking, and singlehandedly supported a mission Sunday School.

At seventy-five she could pass for sixty, with "quick step, full firm voice, deep laugh, and only slightly grayed hair." In her youth she played tennis and rode horseback, and she never lived a cloistered life, though religion was her chief preoccupation.

In her delightful and charming romances, there remains a constant positive spirit that conquers discouragement, and supports the belief that true love and happiness are born from the worst of trials. Her gift is of understanding — making her characters seem real and her stories true-to-life.

Joanna Paulsen
July 1983

*Life Out of
Death*

Life Out of Death

Afterward Philip Gardley remembered his brother Stephen as he stood at the curb just a minute before it happened. What a pleasant smile had been on his face, and how tall and straight and handsome he had looked! The memory wrenched Philip's heart with a dull never-ceasing pain. Stephen had always been such a wonderful brother, more like a father than a brother to Philip, who could not remember his father.

It happened just after the brothers had completed an important conference arranging for Philip to enter into full partnership in the business which Stephen had built up into phenomenal prominence and success. Philip had finished a leisurely college education, topping it off with a prolonged European trip. They came out of the house together to drive down to the office in Stephen's car which stood in front of their home, and Philip, seeing a girl across the street, called a greeting to her. He stepped out into the road the better to hear what she was saying, his

Panama hat in hand, a gay smile on his lips, the honors
of the partnership in the business resting lightly upon his
irresponsible shoulders.

He glanced back as he stepped out into the road and
caught that last glimpse of his brother standing on the curb
with that look of quiet satisfaction upon his face, as if the
thing he had just done meant the summit of his desire.

Even as Philip called out: "Just a minute, Steve," the
idea touched the back of his mind a bit superficially: "Good
old Steve! I believe this partnership means more to him
than it does to me! He always was an unselfish fellow. I
must buck up and take things more seriously!" He flung
an easy smile behind him, and caught that last vivid impression.

Afterward nobody could describe how it happened. The
street was broad and smooth, with plenty of room everywhere. There was no one in sight either way as Philip
stepped out. An instant later a low-bodied speedy sport
car careened around the corner on two wheels and whirled
madly toward him. Its twelve cylinders merely purred in
the distance, and as it shot forward it gave no warning,
sounded no horn. Only Stephen, standing on the curb, saw
the onrushing danger. He gave one lunge forward and
pushed his brother out of the way, but was struck himself
and crushed by the heavy car as it sped wildly on and
vanished around the next corner, its low-crouched driver
taking no time to look back.

The girl across the street screamed and covered her face
with her hands. Philip, unaware of what had really hap-

pened, bruised and much shaken, highly indignant, gathered himself up to look toward that gallant figure of the brother who had stood smiling just a moment before, and found him gone! And down in the road at his feet lay a mangled limp form with blood streaming from the face. Could that be Stephen?

A crowd began to gather. The frightened mother rushed from the house and knelt in the road beside her son. Some one sent for the police and another sent for the ambulance. They telephoned a doctor, and the hospital. The hysterical girl on the sidewalk, and several neighbors who had witnessed the accident from afar, began to piece the story together. Telegraph wires grew hot with messages. Patrol wagons and motor cycles started on a chase for the automobile that had done the deed. But Stephen Gardley lay white and still upon the bed in the dim hospital room with two doctors and several nurses hovering over him, a white anguished mother kneeling by his side. And Philip Gardley, the gay boyish smile dead upon his stark set face, stood at the foot of the bed gripping the iron railing of the foot board, and watched his brother slowly dying in his stead.

For hours they waited there. It seemed like ages to the brother who had never in his life before had anything hard to bear. Minute by minute, hour after hour, Philip had to go over that scene, always beginning with that picture of his splendid dependable brother standing there waiting for him with that smile of perfect content upon his lips.

He had to reconstruct everything that must have happened, to know all that had passed in his brother's mind in that one swift instant of comprehension and choice. It had to be one or the other of them, and Stephen had chosen to be the victim. There was not time to save them both! It was like Stephen to do it of course. But in the general reckoning of all things Philip recognized how much better it would have been for everyone if he had been the victim. Not better for himself! He shivered as he thought of himself lying there in pain with life slowly ebbing away. He had no conception of any such possibility for himself. Yet Stephen had unhesitatingly chosen death for himself, that he, Philip, gay, irresponsible, selfish, might go on living. And he wasn't worth it! He knew in his heart that practically everyone, even his mother, would think so. Yet he had been left here to live, at such a cost, and Stephen had been stricken out of his course!

The awfulness of it all would roll over him overwhelmingly, till he longed to drop out of sight, out of existence, to call on the rocks and the mountains to hide him from the world that had so loved Stephen.

There was no phase of the terrible occurrence that did not force itself upon him as he stood there, on trembling limbs that threatened to crumple under him, gripping that white iron bar with hands that felt weak as water. It seemed that he grew ages older while he stood there watching that white face, swathed in bloodmarked bandages, those closed eyes, watching his mother's anguish, his own heart wrenched with the imminence of dreadful loss. How was he going to live without his brother?

All his life this brother had been safeguarding him,

supplying him with what he needed, even fulfilling his every fancy, and how carelessly he had accepted it all! How as a matter of course he had taken it as only his due, and asked for more. Yes, and got it too! The expensive car for instance! He had found afterward that the business was in straits just then and Stephen had had to drive a cheap second-hand car to manage the extra expense for him. And then his trip to Europe! And the partnership! Oh, the stabbing pain that shot through him at thought of that! What would the business be with Stephen gone!

Oh, wasn't there something that could be done to save him even now?

Yet when he wildly sought the doctor in the hall and besieged him with questions, he only gravely shook his head, and sent him, desperate, back to grip that iron rail and watch for a possible flutter of those white eyelids. Oh, would there not be at least a word, a look, before he went from them forever?

And then, at last, it came—a look fully conscious, a slow smile of precious understanding and farewell that Philip would carry with him into eternity; a voice, low, vibrant, clear, Stephen's last words:

"It's all right, Phil. You'll carry on!"

A fleeting look of deep love into his mother's eyes, and he was gone!

Stephen was gone!

And he, Philip, was left to carry on!

How that thought came down upon his light and easy soul with crushing meaning! How the boy of a day ago shrank into himself and cried out in protest to a God he did not know. How he went through the interminable days of anguish that dragged themselves so unmercifully slowly until the funeral was over! His white anguished face looked out as from the gloom of the valley of the shadow. People said "How he loved him!" in slow astonished voices, and looked after him wonderingly. No one had thought that he had it in him to love and appreciate his brother so deeply.

But Philip did not hear them, did not see the surprise in their faces. He went the necessary way through those awful days up to the afternoon of the service in a kind of daze, seeing but one thought ever before him. He, Philip, had been a dead man, if Stephen had not died for him! There had been no other possibility! Stephen had chosen to lay his splendid successful life down in his place! Stephen had died that he might live, and therefore it was his place to henceforth die to himself that he might live Stephen's life for him. Stephen was an infinitely better man than Philip knew he ever could be, and now that Stephen was gone and the world could not see him nor know him any more, it was his place to carry on Stephen's life as he had begun it, and it seemed an appalling thing that he was asked to do.

The day of the service Philip sat by his mother, where she had chosen to stay, close by the casket where lay that sweet strong face.

When Philip lifted his grief-filled eyes there across the room sat Enid Ainsley, the pretty girl to whom he had been speaking when the accident occurred. He remembered how she had called a gay nothing across that had made him step nearer to hear her. Perhaps there had been a bit of self-consciousness on his own part as he moved toward her, because he knew that Stephen and his mother did not approve of his friendship with Enid. Yes, he knew that there was a fascination about her. He had owned to himself more than once that he was in love with her; yet now in the revulsion that the great catastrophe had brought she seemed almost an offense sitting there in her becoming costume of deep black. He could not bear to look at her. She seemed the cause of his great loss. He wished she had not come. Why should she weep in that hysterical way? It seemed to him that good taste would have kept her away.

Ah! She was one of the things that must be cut out of his life from henceforth. Stephen would never have companioned with a girl like Enid.

Yet even as he turned away his eyes from looking at the girl it came to him that Stephen would never have felt resentment toward her. He was always full of kindliness even toward those who had injured him.

And of course it was not Enid's fault that he had been standing there in the middle of the road talking to her when the peril came.

He groaned in spirit as the interminable service dragged along. He heard nothing of the comfort it was meant to give. He was thinking of his own lost life. Thinking how he must now fit himself into his brother's place and live his life instead of his own.

He had no impatience toward this idea, no question but

that of course he would do it, no parley with himself whether he could not as well shirk this most uncongenial task. It was something that his inner nature demanded of him. It was just that his own bright gay thoughtless life was dead, ended as thoroughly as if he had been crushed beside his brother there on the street by the murderous car; and he had come into the life of another to live it out.

There might be a time when he could look back and be glad of the splendid foundation which his brother had laid for him to build upon, the best start possible that a young man could have in life. At present he could only be aghast.

He looked at the beautiful dead face in the coffin with a stern mask upon his own, struggling to keep his inner feelings from being seen by the world, for it seemed he was really looking upon his own face lying there among the flowers. Dead, he, Philip Gardley, dead with his brother! He knew he could never be his brother, much as he should try, and yet he must try, and equally he could not be himself because of trying.

The first night after the funeral was agony. Stephen's room empty! He could just remember how when he was a little boy Stephen was away at college for four long years. He seemed a great stranger-hero when he came back. But now it had been so very long that Stephen had been always at home. Grammar school days and high school days and then college for himself, and always that wonderful older brother at home making things go, as his father would have done if he had lived. Why, it hadn't occurred to him that Stephen could ever die, at least not till he himself was an old, old man. Old man! Ah! he drew in his breath sharply. Would he have to live out that long, long life for Stephen? "Carry on!" Those were his last words! It looked so interminable to Philip lying in his bed, with Stephen's room closed, empty. No Stephen in the house ever any more. He to be Stephen now! Incredible thought!

He knew his mother was feeling the emptiness of the house, the agony of loss, too. Her door across the hall stood open. He could hear a soft sob now and then, quickly suppressed.

Stephen would have gone to comfort her if he had been here. He had always been like that. He could dimly remember Stephen comforting his mother when he was a tiny child, it must have been after his father's death, although he could not remember that.

Well, if he was to carry on it was his place now to comfort his mother. Could he do it? He shrank from it inexpressibly. He doubted if he could. She had always comforted him—when Stephen wasn't there to do it. But now he was in Stephen's place and must not let her see how much he needed comfort himself. How old he felt!

He lay there trying to get the consent of himself to go and try to do what Stephen would have done; trying to imagine how one should go about comforting a mother; trying to fall asleep before he had actually decided if he must. But by and by his conscience, or something that an-

swered for conscience in his hitherto gay soul, prodded him
beyond the limits and he stumbled up and across the hall,
entering his mother's room almost stealthily as if he might
change his mind after all.

She had ceased sobbing. Perhaps she was asleep and it
was not necessary. He could see the outline of her head
on the pillow; her frail arm beneath the lacy sleeve was
lifted, holding a handkerchief to her eyes. Then she gave
a soft convulsive breath as of a suppressed moan, and
his conscience drove him across the floor, the while his
soul was suggesting that his mother would probably think
it queer of him to come.

She looked up as he approached the bed, half startled.
The thought menaced him that perhaps she would not
want him. Perhaps she even looked upon him as the cause
of her beloved elder son's death. Just as he had thought of
that girl. Perhaps his mother shrank from him, and could
not love him as she had. The thought went like a sword
through his newly awakened soul, and twisted about painfully. He was standing over her now. Perhaps he should
not have come. He felt abject. Should he go back! But he
could not do that without saying something.

He dropped upon his knee beside the bed, bent over
her, and felt his own tears start like a child. He wanted to
hide his face in her neck and weep, tell her he could not
carry on. Ask her to comfort him as she had always done.

But he was a man! He could not do that! He was to
carry on!

Blindly he groped with his lips and touched her eyelids, wet with tears and then was stung with the thought that Stephen had always kissed her so, on her eyelids, and now he was taking Stephen's place. Oh, he ought not to have done that! Perhaps it would hurt her! What an everlasting blunderer he was! He could never learn to take Stephen's place without hurting. He couldn't be Stephen no matter how he tried! Stephen would not have done a tactless thing like that. He should have kissed her forehead as he had always done, lightly, gaily, or her lips. But no, he had to kiss her eyelids, the very thing that would remind her most of her loss! He wanted to turn and run away to hide in dismay at himself.

But the mother's arm suddenly went round him with the old gentle way she had, and she reached her lips to his and murmured: "Philip! Dear son!" and Philip stole away again awkwardly, embarrassedly. He had done his best, and perhaps she liked it. She seemed to him as usual, yet somehow he knew he had not comforted her, only showed her that he was sorry and that he needed comfort himself. Stephen would have had words about heaven and hereafter. Stephen was that way. Philip groped around in his mind for some form of family tradition called religion that would help now, but nothing came to mind. Heaven seemed very far away and undesirable. One had to go on living and being somebody else. All the gay brightness of life was gone. He had to carry on for someone else.

He went down to the office in the morning with a heavy heart and a stern face. He called his brother's helpers about him and tried to gather up the threads that had been dropped by the head of the establishment, but though he conscientiously sought to understand, and asked many questions most earnestly, his mind seemed a blank. There was something hard and artificial about all that he did. He found himself trying to look older than he was, to appear as Stephen would have appeared.

"He's doin' the best he can," said the old Scotchman who had looked after the building since Stephen was first in business. "He's tryin' hard, but a body can't take the place o' thot mon. *Nae* body can!"

And, although the Scotchman did not know it, Philip heard him, gave him one keen glance, and went back to his office to drop his head upon his desk and groan in spirit. How could he carry on for Stephen? What could he do? What was lacking?

Day after day went by and his heart grew heavier. How could he keep it up? He went gravely from house to office and back again, going through the duties of each day carefully, precisely, becoming more proficient in their technique each day, yet getting no nearer to his goal. When strangers from out of town came in to do business they presently sought out the old helpers instead of the new head. They were missing Stephen and he could do nothing about it. He was making a miserable failure of it all! He was not taking Stephen's place even to his mother. He knew it. He was just Philip, the younger son, and she was grieving alone for Stephen, her dependence!

His mother roused to alarm at last, urged him to go out

among his young friends, invite them home, bring some brightness about the house, but he shook his head.

"No, Mother, I couldn't. I'm done with all that!" he answered gravely to her pleading.

The circle of his friends talked him over.

"He might as well have died," said a young girl bitterly. "He's just like one dead. Or like a stranger! He looks at you from so far away! Whoever would have thought his brother's death would have made him like this? He can't bring Stephen back by acting like the tomb!"

And one day he heard two elderly men conversing. They did not know their voices carried to the seat behind them in the suburban train.

"Yes, he's settled down more than I ever dreamed he could," said one, a noted lawyer, whom he knew as a dear friend of his dead father. "I'm sure he's going to make a good man. He used to be a bit wild, but he seems to have given all that up. But he'll never be half the man his brother Stephen was!"

"Oh, no!" said the other who was a wealthy business man and also an officer in the church he and his mother attended. "He lacks something. I wouldn't exactly say pep! He's taken hold of his business with a stern rigidity I wouldn't have expected of one so unstable as he was, but he lacks that deep vital spark that Stephen had, that was almost spirituality even in business matters."

"Yes," said the lawyer thoughtfully, "Stephen was the most Godlike man I ever knew. For so young a man it was most remarkable. It was almost as if Christ were come

down and were living His life for Him. He fairly radiated
God in his whole contact with the world."

Philip sat listening behind his sheltering newspaper and
let the thought drive deep into his heart. It carried real
conviction with it. That was the matter with him. He was
not Godlike. Stephen had been Godlike and he never could
be. He was sure of that! It wasn't in him. Yet somehow, if
he knew how to go about it, he would like to try.

When a mere boy in his teens he had joined the church.
In a general way he had known himself for a sinner and
admitted belief in the atoning sacrifice of the Saviour. It
seemed a kind benevolent thing for the Saviour to have
done to die on the cross in a general atonement, and he
always felt that if there was some mistake about it and it
should prove not to be true, it was at least "a peach of a
fake," and a pleasant way to get through life to have a
safe feeling about the hereafter. But he had scarcely given
two thoughts to the matter since he united with the
church. He felt that he had done all that was necessary,
and there remained but to live a fairly decent life and
he would be eligible for any crowns that were to be handed
out. Now, however, as he thought of Stephen and of what
these two respected men had been saying, he saw that there
must be something more. Stephen had been Godlike. Well,
then *he* would be Godlike too! He would get to work and
get to himself some real righteousness such as Stephen had.

To that end he suggested to his mother that they go to
prayer meeting that night. Much surprised she assented and
they went, but he got very little help from that save a mild

kind of self-satisfaction that he had gone. An old prosy deacon took the service and droned out worn platitudes that did not reach beyond the surface.

But there was mention of a new leader for the Boy Scouts, as the old leader had resigned, and volunteers were called for. Philip thought it over and offered his own services. Perhaps this was the way to become Godlike, to make himself what Stephen had been and make his life tell for the things that had meant so much to Stephen.

They told him that a Sunday School class of boys went with the Scout organization and after a moment's hesitation he took that over too. This was what Stephen would have been likely to do.

He wondered what he should teach those boys. He prepared some platitudes and realized hopelessly the boys' restlessness. The empty words he was giving them meant nothing, had no aim. They were letting them roll off their well-armored young souls like a shower of harmless shot. He wasn't getting anywhere. They didn't even like him very well. He could see that.

For weeks he went on dragging himself through duties, financial and spiritual, getting nowhere. Each week when a meeting was over he resolved to resign before the next, yet went on for Stephen's sake.

Someone asked him to address the Sunday School on Boys' Day because Stephen had always had such a wonderful message for the boys. He tried to do it, but saw through their politeness how bored they were. He had nothing to give them but chips, more platitudes that they already knew

by heart. He was really giving them some of the same old
dry phrases he had hated so in speakers when he was a boy.

That night he got down upon his knees and wept in the
dark. He actually spoke to God and told Him he was a
failure; that he couldn't go on any longer; that God, if
there was a God, who expected him to carry on, must help!
He couldn't do another thing alone!

And then, almost as an answer there came the idea of
going to the minister for help. The minister had never
struck him as being a man to whom one could easily go
in trouble. He was a conservative, elderly, rather formal
man, but a minister *ought* to be able to help in a case like
this, oughtn't he? He was supposed to help the soul to
God, wasn't he? And Stephen had always respected him.

So, late at night, almost midnight it was, he took his
hat and went out, walking down the street on what to
him seemed a very hopeless errand. But it was a last resort.

A stranger opened the door, a younger man than the
minister, a man with disarming eyes and a burr on his
tongue that came from across the water. Philip liked him.
His eyes had something in them that reminded him of
Stephen.

The stranger explained that the minister had gone out
to see a dying man and he was waiting up for him. He said
the minister might be back soon, and opened the door with
such a friendly warmth that Philip stepped in, the while
wondering at himself for doing it. He was not in a mood
for talking with strangers, and the minister would not
want to be kept up any longer after he got home. He

would better have waited until another time. When he was inside he said so, intending to go home at once. But the stranger who said his name was McKnight looked at him with that disarming smile and said:

"Is there anything that I could do for you? I am a servant of the Lord Jesus also, and shall be glad if there is any way that I can help you."

Philip never knew how it came about. Certainly he had no intention of taking that stranger into his confidence. But he presently found himself sitting in the cosy library telling this man with the holy eyes just what was happening in his life and how unhappy he was.

Just a few questions and the kindly stranger who had amazingly become a friend had the whole story of Philip's life.

"And so, my friend," said the stranger, "your brother was a man who knew the Lord Jesus, and had the power of the resurrection in his life. And you are trying to be your brother without knowing his Lord or having the right to that power! Is that it?"

"I don't know what you mean by the resurrection power," said Philip.

"The resurrection power is the Life Christ brought from the tomb when He rose from the dead," answered McKnight. "It is His life that came out of death—'the life whereby Jesus conquered death'. If you have that power within you, it will enable you to live a life on a higher plane than ordinary living. You want to be Godlike? There is no other power that can make you show forth the God-Man Christ Jesus but the power of His resurrection."

"That's all Greek to me," said Philip with bewildered eyes. "I never learned the language you are speaking."

"Well, I'll put it more simply," said the stranger. "You can't be like a man unless you know him, can you?"

"You can't even if you do know him," said Philip sadly. "I've known my brother all my life, and I've tried my best to be like him, and let his life go on in me, and I find it can't be done."

"But are you quite sure that you knew him?" asked the keen-eyed questioner. "You have found something about him into which you cannot enter, his Godlikeness that people speak of. Did you ever know your brother in this phase of his experience? Did you ever get to know thoroughly his inmost heart on this matter?"

Philip stared, then answered quickly:

"No, I wouldn't let him talk to me about religious matters. I wasn't interested."

"Exactly. Then how could you know him thoroughly, and how could you be like him in that respect if you never went with him through his deepest experiences?"

"I suppose I couldn't," said Philip hopelessly. "Then you think there's no use?"

"No! Oh no! I think there is great use. It is quite true that your *brother's* life can never go on in you, but you *can* know his Christ, Who made your brother Godlike. The Lord Jesus Christ is willing to live His resurrection life through you, if you will, as much as He ever did through

your brother. That is a miracle, of course, but we are
speaking of heavenly things, you see."

"How could one know Christ?" Philip's tone was full
of awe.

"The first step is to accept Him as your own personal
Saviour. When you do that His Spirit takes up His dwell-
ing in you. Then surrender to Him so utterly that you
actually reckon your self-life to have died with Him on
the cross, so that you can say: 'I am crucified with Christ:
nevertheless I live; yet not I, but Christ liveth in me: and
the life which I now live in the flesh I live by the faith of
the Son of God, who loved me, and gave himself for me.'
Isn't that substantially the same thing that you have been
trying to do for your brother, to die to your own life that
the life of your brother might go on in the same channels
it had when he was living?"

"It is," said Philip with dawning comprehension.

"Well, that's all, only put Christ in your brother's place.
It is *Christ* whose life must go on through yours; for I am
sure that is what happened in your brother's life. It was
Christ who was living in him, not Stephen Gardley. And
when his body was crushed it was Christ whose resurrection power was hindered, through having one less human
life to dwell in. Did it ever occur to you that the Lord
Jesus can be seen today only through men and women
who are willing to have self slain with all its old programs,
standards, ambitions, desires, aims, will, and let Christ take
up His abode in them? The world saw Jesus through your
brother because your brother counted himself as crucified

with Him, and was therefore under that promise in Romans 6: 'For if we have been planted together in the likeness of His death, we shall be also in the likeness of His resurrection . . . Likewise reckon ye also yourselves to be dead indeed unto sin but alive unto God through Jesus Christ our Lord.' You see, my friend, the death and resurrection of Christ is the power of God, and you have a right to it in your life if you are willing for this death-union with Christ Himself.

"But it is not to be acquired by any effort of your own. It is only through the death of self that He can come in. There is not room for Him and you both, and the natural man must go because God can do nothing with him. The old sinful nature cannot inherit the kingdom of heaven."

Philip listened in wonder as the way was made plain. He was deeply moved at the stranger's prayer for him, and finally went home to read his Bible.

McKnight had sent him to the story of the crucifixion, and straight through the four gospels he read it, till the scene was printed as vividly on his mind as the death of his own brother. For the first time since Stephen's death Philip lost sight of that blood-stained face lying in the dust of the road, and saw his Saviour hanging on the cross instead. He felt the shame, the scoffs, the insults, quivered at the nails driven in the tender hands and feet, saw the trickling blood from the thorn-crown, the awful spear thrust! Ah! This was the One who had died that he might live *eternally*! And this King of all the earth wanted to live out

His life through him! He was asked to "carry on" for the Saviour of the world!

It was just before daybreak that he turned out his light and knelt beside his open window with the morning star still shining, the dawn creeping softly into the sky, and surrendered to his risen Lord; confessed all his own unworthiness, his vain efforts of the flesh to be like another *man*; laid down himself to die with his Lord and said:

"I am crucified with Thee, Lord Jesus. Nevertheless I live, yet not I, Philip Gardley, but Christ liveth *in* me, and the life which I now live in the flesh I live by the faith of the Son of God, who loved me, and gave Himself for me!"

Then a new day began.

He went downstairs to breakfast with a different look in his face. He bent over his anxious mother tenderly and kissed her. He said:

"Mother, I've found the Lord Jesus, and it's going to be all different now!"

They began to feel it almost at once in the office, and as the days went by.

"That young man is growing like his brother!" one of the office force said.

"He is growing like Jesus Christ!" said an old friend of his father's who happened to be in the office at the time.

"Well, I don't know but you're right," said the first. "That was really what I meant, I guess!" and his voice had a note of awe in it.

But then because the enemy never lets a chance go by to

hinder a new-born soul, Enid Ainsley came into his life
again.

Someone had asked her into the church choir for a special musical festival, for she had a really marvellous voice
and was besides quite decorative, with her gold hair, her
vivid complexion and her great blue eyes. Philip also had
promised to help with the music and Enid managed it
quite easily that he should take her home from the re-
hearsals.

At first he attended her gravely, pleading business and
hurrying away at once, but soon she inveigled him into her
home and tried to bring back the old free and easy cama-
raderie.

She played her part cleverly, leading him on to almost
hope that perhaps she too was changing.

One night he tried to tell her of his own experience and
the new hope that had come into his life. But she flung
away from him.

"Oh, for pity's sake, Phil, aren't you ever going to be
yourself again?" she cried out impatiently.

"I hope not," he said gravely.

"Well, I think it's silly, this trying to be like your
brother! It was well enough to respect his memory for
awhile and all that, but it gets boresome to keep it up.
For heaven's sake snap out of it, and quickly, too."

"I'm not trying to be like my brother any longer," he
said quietly. "I found it was impossible, because, you know,
it wasn't he who was living in him, it was Another."

"What do you mean?"

"I mean the Lord Jesus Christ."

"For heaven's sake!" she turned upon him. "Are you turning religious? Phil Gardley gone religious! Well, that's a great joke. That's *precious!* I'll have to tell the gang."

"No," said Philip steadily. "Philip Gardley hasn't gone religious. Philip Gardley has died! Christ Who died for me is living His life in me. Henceforth it's not to be my life, but His. Enid, this thing is very real to me. It's not a joke. And Enid, I want you to let me tell you about it. I want you to know Him too. Enid, I've been loving you for a long time—"

Then Enid used all her guiles to turn his attention to herself and his love for her.

But Philip gently brought back the subject again and again, urging her to accept his Lord also, until at last she flouted out upon him with a cold hard look on her lovely face.

"I'm tired of this," she said haughtily. "I don't care to share your love with anyone else, even a *God!* You can choose between us. Either you give up this fanatical nonsense or I'm done with you once and for all."

He pleaded with her. He tried to make her understand that the thing had been *done.* That he was no longer in a position to choose. He had died with Christ on that cross long ago! He had given his word! But she only turned from him coldly; and at last he went away, sadly, with a break in his heart.

At home he knelt before his Lord and struggled long. Was earthly love to be denied him? Why could not this beautiful woman be drawn by God's Spirit to love His Lord?

It was a long hard struggle, his will against God's will. But was that dying with Christ? He was startled at the thought.

Worn with the struggle he flung himself upon his bed, and sharply the words of the young Scotchman came back to him:

"It is just in the measure that the 'I' has been crucified in your life, that Christ in the power of His resurrection can be revealed to the world through you."

Torn between his desire to have his own way, and his growing realization of what it might mean to his Christian witness if he married this girl, he dropped finally into an uneasy sleep, his last thought a prayer that God would somehow make Enid what she ought to be, and give her to him.

And then there came to him a vision of Christ, standing there at the foot of his bed, with the print of the nails in His hands, and the thorns upon His brow, looking deep into Philip Gardley's soul.

"You and I died on Calvary together, Philip," He said. "Are you remembering that? And now, if I give you what you are asking for, this girl will come between you and me! Are you prepared for that? Are you *willing* for that? She belongs to the world and cares only for the things of the world. She will not accept me as her Saviour! You will have to choose between us as she has said. You may have your way if you will, but you must understand that it will lead you through distress and sorrow, and although I shall never cease to love you, it will separate you and me in our walk together. It will also prevent you from showing my resurrection power to the world. The world will not be able to see me through you if you choose this way. Can you not trust me that this is not best for you?"

He awoke startled, and the struggle went on, but at last he yielded, kneeling low before his Lord and crying out:

> "At Thy feet I fall,
> Yield Thee up my all,
> To suffer, live or die,
> For my Lord crucified."

Out into the world he went, a different world, where a closed door had utterly changed his course. And one day he found a bit of a poem in a magazine, lying on a desk in a room where he had to wait for an interview:

> "Is there some door closed by the Father's hand,
> Which widely open you had hoped to see?
> Trust God, and wait—for when He shuts the door
> He keeps the key!"

The days went by and strange things followed. Disaster suddenly surrounded him on every hand. The bank closed that held his financial situation in its grasp. The business went to the wall and he had to begin all over again. There were perils and perplexities everywhere. But still his Christian witness grew brighter. People marvelled at the way he took his testings. He was walking through it all in the daily consciousness of the Presence of Christ as his constant companion. He was able to say as the days went by, each bringing its new problem:

> "I do not ask my cross to understand,
>   My way to see;
>   Better in darkness just to feel Thy hand
>   And follow Thee."

There came a Sunday when he sat in a shadowed seat back under the gallery of the Sunday School room during the review of the Sunday School lesson by the superintendent. Suddenly the superintendent asked a question.

"Children, did any of you ever see anybody who made you think of Jesus Christ? Who seemed like what you would expect of Jesus Christ if He were to come back here in visible form?"

A quick eager hand went up, Jimmy Belden, one of Philip's Boy Scouts.

"Well, Jimmy?" said the superintendent.

Jimmy stood up promptly and in a clear voice said:

"Mr. Philip Gardley!"

Then did Philip Gardley bow his head and cover his eyes with his hand, his heart filled with glad humility. God had given him that great honor and privilege of being able to show Christ in some small measure at least, to that one Boy Scout, and perhaps to give him some little idea of what that life was whereby Jesus conquered death! It thrilled him with a joy inexpressible and brought tears of humility to his eyes.

And that night as he stood by his window looking up to the stars and thought of it all, his heart recalled a verse he had read that day:

"He was better to me than all my hopes,
  Better than all my fears,
He made a bridge of my broken works,
  And a rainbow of my tears.
The billows that guarded my sea-girt path
  But bore my Lord on their crest!
When I dwell on the days of my wilderness march
  I can lean on His love and rest!"

The Strange

God

The Strange God

The Brandons had always been active Christian workers even when they were very young. Frank Brandon had been made president of the Christian Endeavor in his church when he was a mere boy; and Emily Fuller of the Epworth League in her church when she was very young. Both of them had sung in the choir, both had been most zealous in county and district work of all sorts. They were always being put on committees either in church or community work, wherever any activity was started along religious lines. Just as soon as anything was decided upon some one would always say:

"We'll get Frank Brandon interested in that and it will be sure to go like wildfire," or, "Put Emily Fuller in charge of that and there won't be a hitch in your arrangements."

And so when these two joined forces in marriage every one was marveling over their future and the respective Fuller and Brandon contingents each began planning to absorb them both.

This of course was most pleasant and flattering to them
and the result was that finally each took over many of the
activities of the other, and became busier than ever, abound-
ing in good works, with scarcely time to call their souls
their own. But they seemed to enjoy it. They continued
to take on new activities until one wondered how they did
it. But they never complained of being weary. They seemed
to thrive on the adulation of their friends.

"Oh, you two! You're simply tireless, aren't you?" an
elderly member would say, shaking an admiring finger at
Emily playfully, and sighing lazily. "You'll certainly have
a lot of stars in your crown! I wish I were as good a Christian as you are! You'll certainly have your reward in
heaven! How *do* you *do* it?"

"Oh, that's nothing!" Emily would say lightly, "I just
love this kind of work. But dear Mrs. Brown, *are* you
going to make us one of your marvelous angel cakes for
the sale? And *would* it be too much to ask for two quarts
of your celestial salad besides? You know if your name is
on anything we can charge half again as much and get
away with it. We do want to make enough to get a new
church carpet. The old one is simply unspeakable!"

Mrs. Brown would always end by promising both angel
cakes and salad, and patting Emily on her exquisitely
rouged cheek, saying, "What a wonderful little Christian
you always were, Emily; I quite envy you your crown!"
And Emily would dimple and smile and flutter across the
aisle to beg Mrs. Peters for four quarts of her "heavenly

mayonnaise" to put up in cunning little amber jars with her name hand-painted on the label.

It was just the same with Frank. "Frank, old man, we're putting on a minstrel show to help out with the mortgage on the church this year, and we want you for end man. Now there's no use in making excuses, for there's nobody who can put over the jokes the way you can, and we mean to have you."

Or the Sunday School superintendent would accost him. "Brandon, how about your taking that class of boys? They've had five teachers and finished them all, and the one they have now isn't a teacher at all. He just sits and lets them walk all over him. You could manage them, I'm sure. Get them interested in some class activity; basketball, or tennis, or something athletic, and make them feel some church responsibility. They can join the church leagues and play with other churches, win cups and things, that'll give them a church spirit! Why, those fellows ought all to be church members at their age! How'd it be if you make a rule that only church members are eligible to play in the inter-church games? Something like that, see? I'm sure you'd be just the one to start it."

"Good idea!" said Frank pleasantly. "I'm not sure but I'd enjoy that if I can make the time. I can see possibilities. We could have week-end conferences in the summer up at one of the camps and teach them the latest methods of church work; raising money, etc. and give them a dash of church history, or maybe a talk or two on personal responsibility; something really serious. Then when they get home let them put on a church social, using some of the methods they've learned. We could give two or three prizes; one for the most original program, one for the best suggestion of how to raise money for the church, and—well—one for the best menu for a church banquet. Yes, I can see great possibilities. I'll think it over and try to make time for it. It sounds great to me!"

Things had been going on like this for several years. Frank had a great Bible class of boys—very many boys and very little Bible; and Emily had a like class of girls, whose chief business it was to get up new and startling ways of entertainment to hold the boys in the church. Visiting strangers, introduced to the Brandons and informed how wonderful they were, would respond with a wistful wish that they had some such workers in their church.

The church the Brandons attended was the most thoroughly programmed of any church in the city. The minister was wont to boast that the young people of his church had no need to go anywhere else for their entertainment, they had enough at home.

"Sorry, brother," Frank Brandon said when Harry Sharpless, an earnest young man from another church who was formerly a member of Frank's Bible Class, suggested their joining in a city-wide movement for weekly Bible study. "Sorry, but we wouldn't have time to spare. Monday and Thursday nights we have our regular league games; Wednesday night we have practice in our own church gym. Of course that doesn't come till after the prayer meeting, but it breaks into the evening and no one would like taking on another date for we require them to be on time at practice. Of course the young people don't go to prayer meeting, but to tell the truth some of them get into the gym while prayer meeting is going on and have a little practice on the side, so that hour wouldn't be available. Then Tuesday night our church orchestra and choirs meet, and a lot of our young folks belong to those. Friday night we have either movies or some kind of church entertainment, and Saturday nights we have our church "Get Together Club". Ever hear about that? It's quite unique. We have the whole church divided into sections and they take turns being hosts and hostesses. We have a supper connected with it, of course. We've just put in a miniature golf course in the basement of the church. The young people did the work themselves, and it's great! The old people sit around the fire and sing popular songs and the young folks play games. We have a couple of ping pong tables too. It's really great. Ever been over to see it? You ought to come. Of course we have a modest charge for outsiders to come and play. But I'd be glad to have you come as my guest some time. You'd enjoy it and maybe get an idea of how to work something like it in your church. No, I'm sorry, Harry. I'm afraid we wouldn't be able to join you in that Bible study idea. And you see we really don't need it. Our young people are all hard at work in the church and of course most of them come from Christian homes and we get plenty of that sort of thing on Sunday anyway."

It was the winter that they were putting on the mission-

ary play that Emily stopped Rose Altar, a newcomer to
the church, and asked her to come to a committee meeting
that was to be held in the church parlor an hour before
the morning session of Sunday School next Sunday.

"I'm sorry," said Rose, "I'm afraid I couldn't come at
that time. You see, we always have family worship at that
hour. Sometimes during the week we have to be hurried,
but Father likes to take more time for it Sundays."

"Family worship! How quaint!" said Emily staring a little. "Imagine it! I didn't know anybody did that any more.
But couldn't you stay away just once? You see, we're putting on a marvelous play next month and we're assigning
the characters. We want to begin to rehearse this week because we want to take all the time possible for preparation,
and we thought we could just read over some of the parts
and let you get the idea, and see what you were expected to
do. We'd do it in the afternoon only the church orchestra
is giving a sacred concert then and a good many of us are
in that. But anyhow, can't you come just this once? Tell
your father it's *quite* religious. It's a sort of a pageant of
all missionary lands. The costumes are gorgeous! They are
ordered from abroad. The Mission Board is getting them
for us. There's a dear little Mohammedan one that I think
would about fit you. I know you would be stunning in it.
We are hoping to do a lot of good with this play. It's the
beginning of the great World Drive for Foreign Missions,
you know, and it's marvelous what a prospect we have.
We've already had three invitations to put the play on at

other churches. If all goes well we rather expect to give it a good many times, in the suburbs, and even over in the next state. I wanted to be sure and get you to come in with us right at the start, for I have an idea you'll be awfully good."

But Rose Altar shook her head.

"I'm sorry, Mrs. Brandon, you're very kind, but I just haven't time for things of that sort."

"Oh, I'm sorry," said Emily a bit shortly.

She was stung and astonished that the sweet young stranger had not immediately recognized and followed her lead. She was not used to having any one refuse her requests and invitations.

"Poor child," she said to herself, looking after her with an almost contemptuous smile. "She must be under the domination of a fanatical father. Fancy family worship! How quaint! How Victorian! Well, she'll come around of course when she sees it's the thing to do, but she'll have to take what is left. I can't run any risks waiting. She can be a Zulu girl, of course, if nothing else is left, though she may object to the bead costumes. However—I've done my best for her."

So the play went on and enthusiasm spread like wildfire.

The Bible study classes went on also, and many unexpected ones were added to them—of such as should be saved. But there was a large number of eager, earnest young church members who would have come into the Bible meetings and enjoyed them, but they felt their first duty was toward the mission play that their own church was getting up. It was going to do so much good for foreign missions!

Frank Brandon, coming home from his office an hour later than usual one day in late February, swung himself aboard the train just as it was starting, and walked through three crowded cars finally dropping into the only vacant seat he could find, the little single one by the door. He opened the evening paper. He was extremely tired and didn't want to talk, for things had not gone well. The first thing that morning his valued secretary had sent word her mother was very sick and she couldn't come to the office that day. He had been obliged to hire a public stenographer. Then about ten o'clock word had come that the bank where he kept his prosperous account had closed its doors, cutting him off indefinitely, not only from his bank account, but also from the safety deposit box, which contained valuable papers and bonds which might be used for collateral. Besides he had a headache and a sore throat and ached all over. His throat had been sore when he left home that morning in the sleet and slush, having forgotten his rubbers in his haste. He shivered as the draught from the opening and closing car door slithered down his collar. He felt miserably sick and remembered he had a meeting of the federated committees in the church that evening. He unfurled a newspaper more as a protection than because he wanted to read it. He didn't want to talk to anyone. He was not noticing his fellow passengers. His eyes were on his paper, though he was not much interested in its news. The usual number of accidents, murder cases, and a new suicide, Mather, director of the bank where his money had been. Well, what good did that do, committing suicide? Coward! Thinking to slip out of his obligations that way and leave the mess to other people! Well, of course the man wasn't even a church member. He hadn't any respect for himself. You couldn't expect a man like that——

Suddenly he forgot to finish his thought for he heard his own name spoken by one of the two men sitting just in front of him. He hadn't noticed who they were, but now he recognized their voices. One was Mr. Harris, a successful lawyer, as noted for his interest in church affairs, as he was in his profession. The other was Harry Sharpless. It was Harris who spoke first:

"Did that man Brandon from the Fifth Church go into your Bible Conference work?"

"No," said the other, "he said he hadn't time!"

"Why, I'm surprised," said Harris. "I supposed he was a live wire, always interested in church affairs. With such speakers and teachers as you have secured I would have expected him to *take* the time!"

"Haven't you ever noticed," said young Sharpless with a bit of a twinkle, "that Frank Brandon never goes in for anything that he himself isn't running? He just has to be the head or he won't play. And from all I've seen his wife must be a good deal the same way. It's a case of:

'I love me! I love me!
I'm wild about myself!
I love me! I love me!
My picture's on my shelf!"

"Well, I don't know but that's so," said the graver voice
sadly. "I hadn't thought about it before. Too bad, isn't it?
He could be such a power. Do you know, Sharpless, there
are a great many self-worshippers today who are going
about most actively carrying on service in their own
strength, and for their own sakes. They worship self under
the impression that they are worshipping God. That is the
blinding of the enemy, a part of the great delusion. Power,
success, without God! When all the time the Lord is saying: 'Not by might, nor by power, but by my spirit, saith
the Lord of hosts!'

"What a pity Brandon couldn't be present at some of those
meetings. Even one would be an eye-opener to him, for I
believe that at heart he is a conscientious young man, if he
could only be made to see the truth."

Frank Brandon shrank further behind his paper. Cold
angry chills ran down his back, a sick feeling came in the
pit of his stomach. His feet and hands were like ice and
his face burned hot with fury. Was this what people
thought of him? Was it possible that they so misjudged
him? Admired and successful though he had been, generous
and ready to help everybody, yet there were those who
thought of him like that! Of course it was jealousy. A man
couldn't expect to be popular and not have some people

jealous of him. But these were Christian people, prominent in church circles! Who would ever have suspected them of such petty jealousy? Well, he was thankful that he had none of that! A scrap from the solo he had sung in church last Sunday rang through his memory:

"God, I thank thee that I am not as other men!
 I fast twice in the week,
 I give tithes of all that I possess!"

And they thought he was an egotist! Both of them actually agreed that he was always thinking of himself. That obnoxious song that Sharpless had quoted! He knew it. He used to sing it in college. His lips shut sternly. It was outrageous!

Well, he would just forget it of course, that was the Christian thing to do. But somehow he must show those two that what they said was untrue. He really couldn't stand having anybody going around talking about him like that! Perhaps it would be a good thing to just lean over and challenge what they had said now, settle the matter right then and there and dominate the situation before those two went out and spread such an idea! That was the only way to handle such a thing. Get them in the wrong, embarrass them, just lean forward and smile and ask them pleasantly—well—just what could he ask them? He couldn't merely get up and declare himself innocent of their charge. If they really had such a thing in the back of their minds, his word that it wasn't so wouldn't mean a thing. What proof could he bring that it wasn't so?

Then like a tantalizing little imp, the couplet ran through his brain.

> "I love me! I love me!
> I'm wild about myself."

And something moved within him. Could it be that there was any truth in the assertion that he wasn't interested in anything that he himself didn't run? Of course people were always asking him to take over the management of so many things. He couldn't help it, could he, that there were so many things he was responsible for that he hadn't time for the rest? There! that was something he could ask those two! He would do it right away and see what they said.

But having made this resolve he suddenly felt that he must have a little more to say.

While he paused to collect a list of his good works wherewith to confound them, suddenly the two rose as one man, with the exclamation: "Why, there is Dr. Leveridge up there at the other end of the car. Let's go and speak to him!" and they hurried eagerly forward to greet a gray-haired, kindly-faced man. Frank recognized him as one who had been pointed out to him a few days ago as a conference speaker.

Frank lowered his paper an inch and watched the eager meeting between the three men. He saw how their faces lighted. He was wont to see faces lighted with greeting like that for himself. Yet two of these faces held behind them thoughts against his reputation as a Christian! Of course Sharpless had been just a kid in his Sunday School class not long ago.

But a sick wave of fury passed over him. Somehow he felt left out, and he was not used to being left out. He couldn't just march down the aisle and tell them he had overheard them talking about him. They hadn't even known he was there! But he could easily get out into the other car now while they were up front and they would never know he had been there. That was of course the dignified thing to do and he had known it all the time, only his fury had made him impatient. He would go at once while they had their backs turned. He arose swiftly and slipped out the door, crossing the platform to the next car.

There were no seats in the next car and Frank had to stand on the platform by the door swaying with the train and hiding his face with his newspaper. But it was a salve to his hurt feelings to know that there were several younger men in that aisle ahead of him who would eagerly have urged him to take their seats while they stood in the aisle or sat on the arm, hanging on his words, if they had known he was there. But he was not ready to talk with any one just now. He had just received the shock of his life. It had never before entered his head that any one *could* talk that way about him. He felt a righteous wrath, with a great pity for himself, and he must get himself adjusted and know what to do next before he talked with any one, even Emily.

He decided not to tell Emily anything about it. No need of her having to bear this, too. Of course young Sharpless had been the only one of the two who had said anything really mean. That awful song—"I love me!" It disgusted him more and more as he thought of it. What Lawyer Harris had said wasn't so bad, only he had in a way accepted the slur. Christian people! Talking that way about one who was doing twice as much Christian work as they were!

Well, somehow he must prove to them that they were wrong. How would it do to go to one of their old meetings? Let himself be seen in a front seat! Make it known that he was in thorough sympathy, only he had not been able to go sooner! That was a good idea. If he could get rid of this rotten headache and the aches all over him, he would go tonight. Of course there was a meeting of the federated committees tonight, but it wasn't important, and he could telephone to Sommers to take his place as chairman for once. Well, he would do it no matter how bad he felt! It was important to reverse this feeling before everyone heard of it.

When the train stopped at his station he swung off into the darkness hurrying down the street to his home. He didn't take a taxi lest someone else would be in it. He didn't want to talk with anyone. His throat was raw and his head throbbing. He drew his collar up about his neck and bent his head against the wind and sleet. He knew he was in no condition to go out again that night, but he meant to go. It rather gave him satisfaction that he was going in spite of being sick. It had come to seem quite the most important thing in the world that he be seen in the front seat of the conference *at once*.

At home Emily protested:

"Why, you are *sick*, Frank, and it's beginning to sleet! You're not fit to go out. Besides, you have that committee meeting. I was going to suggest that you call them up and have them meet here. Then we could ask their wives and serve coffee and cake afterward. I think that would be much more interesting."

"No," said Frank, "I've got to go to that conference tonight! I promised I'd look in on them and this is perhaps the last night! Anyhow it's important. There are reasons why I feel that I should lend my influence to it. And I'd like you to go along with me if possible! I really feel we ought! I find it's quite expected of us, and I guess it must be a good thing. They need encouragement. Poor things. They've got that great hall on their hands and I don't suppose it'll be half filled. We really should have gone earlier, taken hold of the thing somehow. It seems people think *we* ought to do *everything*!"

So they went to the meeting. When they turned into the street where the hall was located they wondered if there was a funeral somewhere, there were so many cars parked on both sides of the street. They had to go a block and a half away from the hall and walk back, and Frank had forgotten his rubbers again.

When they reached the hall, they were surprised to find people pouring in by the hundreds. They thought at first they must have got in the wrong place.

And there was no front seat to be had! Indeed there was
scarcely a seat left anywhere on the street floor, and the
galleries were filling fast. Men were already standing
leaning against the walls. So Frank found a place for Emily
behind a post where practically no one could see her, while
he stalked up the aisle and took up his stand on his angry
aching limbs at one side of the pulpit steps. He leaned
against the cold, cold wall, and presently discovered there
was a cold air ventilator right over his head that blew
down his neck. But anyone who could see the platform
could not fail to see him standing there, one foot braced
on the lower step of the pulpit. There he stood with a
haughty heart but a smile of patronage locked upon his
face for the evening.

It was hard work standing there with his whole body
aching like the toothache. The room was hot, for the audience was vast, and he was constantly conscious of his hot,
dry, prickly throat. But as he gazed into the faces of that
audience he forgot his own discomforts. In amazement he
noticed people present who seldom attended any church.
He wondered how they got them there? There hadn't been
any special advertising! And there were families, *whole*
families, from all the churches, eagerly uniting in singing
with a zest that showed they counted it a special privilege
to be there. This really was something that he ought to have
recognized, it seemed. Yet failing to find a response from
him, the Lord had done it without him! He felt somehow
aggrieved at God.

The singing astonished him right at the start; it was so

tremendous, and the congregation didn't need to be worked up to it, either. There was an earnest man up on the platform holding them all in perfect time with an unobtrusive hand. He had a cultured voice with heart-throbs in its very timbre, but he seemed to be merely directing the great volume of sound that was not perfunctory, but came from hearts alive and singing unto the Lord.

Frank Brandon had conducted choruses himself that had been considered great successes. He had always felt he could bring out of an audience the utmost sound it possessed. But he had never heard such singing as this in his life. As they started on the second hymn, which was eagerly requested from the audience, he found there were tears in his eyes. But the words were almost startling. They were:

"Empty me of self, Lord Jesus," ——

He looked around furtively, half wondering if Sharpless or Harris had called for it. He felt once more that sharp stab of query. *Was* he a self-willed man without knowing it?

The tide of song swept about him thrilling him with its greatness, and bringing a strange wistfulness that he might have been a part of all this from its inception. Then with his newly-awakened senses he questioned keenly, was that pang he felt jealousy? He put that aside to think about later for a man with a marvelous voice was singing a solo, not merely showing off his glorious voice, but singing a message to souls:

"Not I, but Christ, be honored, loved, exalted;
Not I, but Christ, be seen, be known, be heard;
Not I, but Christ, in every look and action,
Not I, but Christ, in every thought and word.

"Christ, only Christ, no idol ever falling;
Christ, only Christ, no needless bustling sound;
Christ, only Christ, no self-important bearing;
Christ, only Christ, no trace of 'I' be found.

"O to be saved from myself, dear Lord,
O to be lost in Thee,
O that it might be no more I,
But Christ, that lives in me."

The words sank deep into his soul, and added to his discomfort. Up there in the shadows of the vaulted ceiling somewhere above the gallery he seemed to feel a Presence whose eyes were searching him through and through!

But the voice of the preacher broke in upon his thoughts. It was the Dr. Leveridge whom Harry Sharpless and Lawyer Harris had met so eagerly on the train! Frank looked up, prejudiced against him already, and studied the kind strong face, the fine head crowned with silver hair, the keen eyes. But in spite of his prejudice he could not but admire the cultured voice of the speaker as he announced his text:

"If we have forgotten the name of our God, or stretched out our hands to a strange god; shall not God search this out? for he knoweth the secrets of the heart."

The verse was utterly unfamiliar to Frank Brandon and startled him as if the words had been spoken for him alone. It reached even to joints and marrow and divided the very soul and spirit of him. It seemed to Frank Brandon that he had never heard a verse of scripture before that so searched his being. He wondered in his astonishment where the preacher had found such a verse. He did not remember having heard it before. Some new translation probably! But it gave him for the first time in his life the consciousness of God searching out his innermost secrets. God right there looking into his thoughts! A great panic swept over him, causing him to really doubt whether God would find everything in him entirely satisfactory. Was he, after all, quite as letter-perfect as he had always supposed himself? This sudden amazing jolt to his usually complacent spirit, added to the discomfort of his body, made his situation almost unbearable. He indignantly put away such thoughts and set his lips to smile approbation. His whole attitude and expression ought to show keen interest and enjoyment. He must carry this through to the end at all odds.

The preacher swept on with a discourse that burned into his soul with a new kind of torture. He began by speaking of things that go toward making a soul forget God. Prominent in the list he mentioned great Christian activity, especially the kind in which men make a plan and ask God to bless it, rather than waiting on the Lord to discover what He would have done. He tore the halo from the Christian who is immersed in this sort of man-planned activity by holding up to view a Lord whose very love constrains the heart to look to Him and "lean not to its own understanding."

Frank Brandon listened in amazement to a doctrine he had never heard even hinted at before. He knew in his honest heart that nearly everything that he had ever done in the name of Christ had been after this sort and if this were true he was being condemned. He tried to reason against it all, to protest in his soul, but the preacher was backing up every word he said with a verse of scripture.

Then the preacher went on to speak of strange gods that men commonly set up in their souls. Money, Pleasure, Worldly Amusement, Fleshly Lust——

Ah! Frank lifted up his head triumphantly. None of these were enshrined in his heart. Of that he was very sure. He had lived a clean life, he had no time for worldly amusement, or personal pleasure, and he was not especially fond of money. Look how well he had behaved that morning when the bank closed! He had always given largely of what he possessed. He did not feel condemned in any of those ways.

But now the speaker had come to another god, the commonest one, he said, the one most often enshrined in the human heart. That was Self. Self-will, self-esteem, having one's own way, the desire to dominate, even over God Himself, and bend His way to our will.

He went into the matter most fully and keenly. Like a surgeon using the scalpel of the Word of God he laid bare Frank Brandon's true self to his own eyes. He saw himself by his very activities putting God out and himself in, getting praise to himself instead of God; actually singing praises to himself. That heathenish little verse flashed through his harried mind.

> "I love me! I love me!
> I'm wild about myself!"

He began to see that his very attendance tonight at this strange meeting had been for the worship of Self, an attempt to put Self back on its pedestal before the world.

In closing the speaker brought out the fact that this self-worship was the sin of Satan who once was Lucifer, son of the morning, the anointed cherub, until iniquity was found in him. Satan's sin was in trying to put himself in God's place. The speaker quoted the awful condemnation:

"How art thou fallen from heaven, O Lucifer, son of the morning! how art thou cut down to the ground, which didst weaken the nations!

"For thou hast said in thine heart, I will ascend into heaven, I will exalt my throne above the stars of God: I will sit also upon the mount of the congregation, in the sides of the north:

"I will ascend above the heights of the clouds; I will be like the most High.

"Yet thou shalt be brought down to hell, to the sides of the pit!"

From then on Frank Brandon was engrossed in his task of heart-searching until they began to sing in closing that hymn of consecration:

"Have Thine own way, Lord! Have Thine own way!
Thou art the Potter, I am the clay.
Mould me and make me after thy will,
While I am waiting yielded and still."

He knew those words. He had taught them to many an audience. He had always urged them not to drag. "Make it snappy!" he used to say. Never before had the words meant a thing to him. Now they thrilled through him like an alien prayer in which his lips were forced to join, but his soul was full of wild rebellion, struggling to keep Self on its shrine.

He did the proper thing at the close of the meeting: shook hands with the preacher and those active in the conference; told them how sorry he was that his other dates had prohibited his being present at every session, said how wonderful the meeting had been, and how much he knew he had missed; told them to count on him for anything he could do to keep up the spirit of the conference; explained how he was president of this, chairman of that, leader of the other, his time so filled that he could scarcely ever do anything extra. And then suddenly he realized that nobody was listening to him. Nobody seemed to have noticed his absence nor to be especially delighted that he was here tonight. They seemed to take it for granted that anybody would be there who could!

Finally with a sick sense that he could not stand much more and ought to be in bed, he hunted up Emily behind her post and hurried home.

Some time in the night he awoke to the knowledge that he was very ill indeed. His body was on fire with fever and yet shivering with cold. His eyes were burning, his head was throbbing, his limbs aching unbearably and his throat swollen almost shut.

Emily was up doing things for him, asking him wearisome questions that he did not want to answer. There were hot-water bags about him and an ice bag on his head. A doctor was there somewhere in the dimness of things. Was that possibly a nurse in the offing? And Emily beside the bed on her knees sobbing—it might even be praying.

It all wearied him inexpressibly and he wandered off into a strange place of fire and ice. He did not want to go but it seemed some duty was compelling him and then he saw before him shrines, his and Emily's. They were like two wooden alcoves on the clear icy pavement, with shelves above a kneeling place, and pictures in costly frames upon the shelves, and haloes over the pictures. He stepped closer to see the picture in his own shrine and found it was a likeness of himself! He was startled to notice what a proud and haughty expression he wore, hard, worldly! Was he like that? And did God search it out and see it? He looked again and now he saw there was sin in his face. Actual sin!

Heartsick he stepped aside to see what picture was in Emily's shrine, and lo, it was not her own likeness that was there, but another picture of his own haughty self with a self-satisfied smile upon his face. He wondered in his fevered brain whether in the eyes of God it was any better for a woman to have her husband in God's place rather than herself? He dimly perceived that they were both strange gods in the eyes of God. Then somehow there seemed to be a compelling force upon him that made it necessary for him to go back to his own shrine and worship. Pray to himself! How could he?

Ah, there were prayers stored up upon the shelf—many of them! High sounding words full of fleshly desires, ending always: "Bless *myself*, *my* work, make all *my* schemes succeed and *my* enemies fail." They seemed so empty now as he took them down and read them over painfully upon his knees.

And now a song of praise to his strange god was required of him, and there was only one song he knew. His voice suddenly shrilled out through the sick room startling the nurse and Emily as they hovered anxiously near at hand. It wasn't the voice wherewith he had charmed audiences with wonderful solos, nor yet the rich tones wherewith he had carried audiences into great tides of song. It was a high, excited, fevered voice shrilling and breaking and fading into nothing:

> "I love me! I love me!
> I'm wild about myself!"

"Oh Frank! *Don't!* *Please* don't!" sobbed Emily, very far away.

"But I *must*, Emily," he protested petulantly. "Don't you see the picture there on my shelf? I *have* to sing:

'I *love me!* I *love* me!
There's my picture-on-my-shelf!' "

His voice suddenly trailed away into silence.

Then he looked up at the picture and saw an astonishing thing. For now the picture, though himself unmistakably, nevertheless had the evilly handsome eyes of Lucifer, son of the morning, and he saw even out of the murk of his delirium that "whoso putteth himself in the place of God" is really putting there Satan, the tempter of the world, the enemy of God, the enemy of the Saviour of the world. And suddenly Frank Brandon knew himself to be a sinner and cried aloud in awful anguish!

"Oh *God!* Forgive! Help! *Help!*"

The nurse thought that he was in pain and gave him a soothing powder till he slept.

But Emily upon her knees beside the bed was praying! She thought that he was dying, and she prayed, *really* prayed, perhaps for the first time in her life.

A long time afterward he awoke in the dim quiet of the sick room. Emily and the nurse were hovering in silence not far away, awaiting the outcome.

Suddenly the hush of the room was broken once more by song.

It was still not the voice with which he had been used to charm audiences, or to conduct choruses so successfully. It was not even the voice with which he had sung that

strange grotesque melody when he was taken sick, or the
voice with which he had cried out to God for mercy when
he saw himself and his own sin. It was a thin high thread
of a voice, burned out with fever, and quavering with weak-
ness.

> "Oh—to—be—saved *from myself,*—dear Lord!
> Oh—to—be—lost *in Thee!*
> Oh—that it might be—*no—more*—I,
> *But Christ*—that lives—in—me!"

At the first breath Emily crept to his side and knelt, slipping her hand into the thin white hand that lay so feebly
on the coverlet. But the feeble fingers held her own in a
weak pressure, and the shadow of a smile trembled over
his lips as he said faintly, pausing for breath:

"Isn't that what we want it to be, dear,—from—now—on?
Christ—in—us?"

"Oh, yes," she answered softly, "just His will! Frank,
dearest, do you know, it was not until I handed you over
to Him, and prayed 'Not my will, but Thine be done,' that
He gave you back to me, and you began to get better."

It was very quiet in the room while a soft understanding passed from one hand to the other, and then tenderly
two voices instead of one quavered out into the silence
again.

> "Have Thine own way, Lord, have Thine own way!
> Hold o'er my being absolute sway!
> Fill with Thy Spirit till all shall see
> Christ only, always, living in me!"

The nurse was standing just outside the door listening to see if she would be needed, and now she turned away with a strange mistiness in her eyes, saying softly to herself:

"Well, those two must have been real after all! I didn't think they were!"

The Handmaid
of the Lord

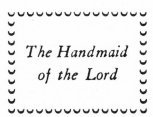

The Handmaid
of the Lord

It was long past midnight and the city of Jerusalem was sleeping. Even the far dim stars seemed to have withdrawn, and a great silence was abroad, as if the earth were waiting for some momentous catastrophe that was to break on the morrow.

Down a narrow dark street in the more crowded portion of the city a stealthy figure walked, drawing his rough coat about him and shivering as he stole along, watching each cross street furtively either way and skulking out of sight into a doorway whenever other pedestrians appeared. He was startled even at a gaunt dog that stalked across his pathway; he drew out of sight until the dog was gone.

Halfway down the street he paused before a plain insignificant house tucked between two larger ones. Slipping close, he stood a moment listening, cautiously peering

around the corner of an arched doorway into a paved passage between the houses, and then gave three taps twice
repeated upon the door. Though they were cautiously
given, yet they re-echoed throughout the narrow street, and
the visitor withdrew into the covered passage and kept
watch until he heard one coming to open the door.

Presently a crack of light appeared beneath the door,
and a glimmer in the lattice above. A low voice demanded
who was there.

For answer, the visitor tapped rhythmically with the tips
of his fingers a bit of code that seemed to be understood,
for the door was opened a crack, and a woman's voice
asked once more, "Who is it?"

"Is Mary, the wife of Joseph, staying here?" asked the
stranger sidling closer to the door.

"She is resting now," explained the woman in a guarded
tone. "She has had a hard evening. I have persuaded her to
try to sleep. Perhaps in the morning she can see you."

"I must see her at once," demanded the stranger gruffly.
"It is important!" and he slid a foot within the crack of
the door and looked furtively behind him up and down
the dark street.

"Is it—about—?" the woman lowered her voice to a whis-
per.

"Yes!" said the man. "About her Son. Jesus! Won't you call her?"

"Oh! has something more happened?" The woman's hand went to her heart.

"Plenty!" said the man harshly. "Let me come in. It is not well that I should be seen here. I must speak with Mary at once. Make haste for the time is short!"

He pushed roughly inside the door and made it fast behind him.

"Who?" asked the woman peering into the dark face by the light of the tiny lamp which she held high, whose wick was almost spent. "Who shall I say is come?"

"No matter!" said the man turning his face into the shadow. "Tell her it is one of His friends."

"I do not think I have met you," the woman hesitated. "I have been with her all the evening."

"Won't you make haste?" snapped the man roughly. "It matters not who I am. I bring her important news. I must see her at once! If you will not call her, I shall search the house for her. I have no time to trifle."

With a frightened glance back of her, the woman turned and hurried into an inner room, leaving the lamp blinking upon the table beside the man, who stood impatiently tapping his sandaled foot on the earthen floor.

There was a sound of low voices, a frightened exclamation, and then hurried steps in the next room. The door
was opened, and Mary stood in the room, a look of fear
on her delicate, exquisite features. Her hands were clasped
convulsively over her heart as if with terrible premonition,
traces of recent tears were upon her pale cheeks, her eyes
were large with anxiety as she peered into the shadows of
the room to see the man who stood lowering beside the
door. Then she stepped nearer and lifted the lamp to throw
the light more freely on his features.

Suddenly she put down the lamp upon the table, her face
hardened into scorn and indignation.

"You?" she exclaimed in a low, challenging voice. *"You!
Judas!* You *dared* to come to me?"

The man cringed angrily into the shadow and put up a
hand to stay her speech.

"Listen!" he said gruffly, "I have words to speak to you!"

"And why should I listen to you?" asked Mary in a clear
tone that could be heard distinctly by her friend at the
door of the inner room. "If there were some news of Him,
could they not have sent a *friend* and not an enemy? If
He is dead, Judas, *you* have killed Him! You, who pre-
tended to be one of His most earnest followers! I know

what you have done! I have heard it all from an eye-witness!"

"He is not dead," said Judas sullenly, "and I have done nothing but what should have been done. What I did, I did for His sake!"

"For *His* sake!" said Mary contemptuously. "You betrayed Him with a *kiss*!" Her voice was hot with scorn.

"I did it for His sake!" persisted Judas. "The time had come when, if He was to be placed upon the throne, He must be made to manifest His power and show what He was and what He could do. Just little miracles were not enough any more. There must be some great public manifestation. I was sure that when He saw that He was hopelessly in the hands of His enemies, with soldiers surrounding Him, He would be forced to manifest His power and show them that He was what He claimed to be. If He had passed through their midst and disappeared, got out of their hands miraculously, there are many who would have believed on Him at once. It would have been nothing then to have gathered an army and put Him immediately upon the throne. But now—!"

"But now?" repeated Mary, her eyes bright with scorn, her lips thin with anguish and indignation.

"Well, now He simply left us in the lurch!"

"Left *you* in the lurch? What do you mean?"

"Why, you understand of course," answered the man, "that if we put Him on the throne we naturally expected some pretty good offices in the new Kingdom. But He seems to have forgotten all about that, just left us in the lurch!—failed us miserably. He has let Himself be drawn into a terrible strait. He simply played into their hands. I can only think He had been asleep and did not realize —or—perhaps He is figuring even yet to perform some greater miracle, break the bands that bind Him, and show the world what He is; but He has gone too far! He does not seem to realize what power the Sanhedrin has. He simply lost His nerve and went with them as quietly as if it were nothing, without a word of protest! He thinks, I suppose, that He will be able to argue them out of it with wise words. But things have gone too far for that. It is too late for that sort of thing. Something must be done at once or there is no hope left. They have taken Him to Pilate! And Pilate dare not be friendly! He has too much to lose!"

"To Pilate!"

Mary stepped back with a quick convulsive pressure of her hand upon her heart, new anguish in her eyes, and reeled as if she would have fallen, had not her friend Salome stepped from the doorway and put a steadying arm about her.

Then Mary rallied and her eyes flashed fire.

"They have taken Him to Pilate! My Son! My Holy One! And you stand here, you who are responsible for it, to prate and excuse yourself and say you did it for His sake! Stand aside! Don't waste my time further! I must go to Him!"

"That is what I have come here for, to take you to Him," answered the man. "But first, I must tell you something. There is something you can do, a way to save Him if you will."

Mary turned upon him quickly.

"What do you mean, something *I* can do? When *you* have done your worst? And who are *you* to tell *me* how to save Him? Am I to pay you thirty more pieces of silver to have you use your tainted influence to save Him after you have sold Him for your own gain? You traitor! You who sold your Lord for silver! Would you also ask more silver of me, His anguished mother?"

"You do not trust me!" whined the man. "I swear I come as a friend, yet you do not trust me!"

"No! I do not trust you! Can one trust a traitor?"

"You will not feel so when I have told you what I have

come to suggest," answered the man suavely. "Listen! The
time grows short. Even now Pilate may be on the point of
ordering the soldiers to bring Him forth for trial. The
morning is about to dawn. Because of the feast, they will
hurry this business through. He will be tried perhaps at
daybreak—early, they said, and I hurried straightway to tell
you. For, Mary, mother of Jesus, you, *you* are the *only*
one who can save Him now! He might have saved Himself if He had chosen, but now He has shown that He
cannot save Himself. There must be found another way.
And I have found it. There is still hope for Him if you
will do one thing. Would you let your Son go to His
death because you would not listen?"

Mary caught her breath in a quick agonized sob, her
eyes aflame with anguish, as she watched her tormentor.

"Oh! *You!*" she cried desperately. "You goad me with
your words till I cannot refuse, though I feel in my heart
you are His enemy! Well, say on! What have you to pro-
pose? I will not have it said that I blindly refused. Speak
quickly! What is there that I can do?"

"Sit down!" said the man trying to put a gentler note
into his cold voice, "you are worn and weary and can listen
better so!"

"I *stand!*" said Mary firmly.

"All right. Have it you own way. Well, then, it is this. You know that the whole trouble centers about His assertion of deity. If that were denied, the matter would be dropped, and the Jews would be appeased. He is arrested because He claims to come from God, to be the expected Messiah. Take that claim from Him, and it would be as easy to get Him released as any common criminal, like Barabbas, for instance."

A long shiver of horror went through Mary as he spoke, but she controlled herself and flashed him a quick scornful look.

"And what has that to do with me?" she asked.

"Everything!" he answered with a kind of satisfaction in his voice. "Because it happens that you are the only one who can take that from Him. This tradition of holiness with which you have surrounded Him, the hint that He is not Joseph's child, makes all the difference in the world. You have only to deny that He is of heavenly parentage, and the trouble will all drop away. And then it will be easy, when He is released, to spirit Him away into the hills for a time, for rest and recuperation from a nervous breakdown, you know, until all be forgotten. Then we can prepare an army secretly, when the trouble has quieted

down and the Sanhedrin is not expecting it, to put Him
upon the throne, and all will yet be well."

"You mean—?" asked the mother with slow, awe-stricken
utterance, and white, horrified lips.

"I mean," went on the assured voice of the man, "that
you are to come forward as His mother and say that He
is really Joseph's child after the flesh; that all this talk
about His being the Messiah is a mistake; that you never
meant people to understand that He was of miraculous
birth. People will believe you. You are well respected here.
And you are the only one in the whole world who rightly
knows His parentage. If you are unwilling to have Joseph
stand as His natural father, then say who *is* His father. A
little blight upon your honor will not matter to you, I
know, against the possibility of His death. And when He
sits upon the throne, it will not matter that you have borne
dishonor for a few days."

Mary was white to the lips. She stood back now with
clenched hands down at her sides, the full light of the
flickering, spent little wick flaring upon her face and light-
ing it with a glow of righteous wrath.

"You mean," and she caught her breath to make her voice
more clear, "you mean that I should *lie* to save my Holy

One from death? You mean that I should make *His own* words *lies?*"

"If it *is* a lie," sneered the man shrugging his shoulders. "Yes, a little lie like that to save a life! It is nothing!"

"It is *every*thing!" proclaimed Mary, her voice suddenly rising in a kind of exultant throb. "It is His very life and being, the purpose for which He was sent into the world! It would mean discrediting the word of angels, and the message from God Himself. It would mean denying the power of the Most High! Destroy His heavenly parentage, and you destroy the Saviour of the world—and make Him a liar and a criminal—or crazy!"

"Call it crazy then!" laughed the man. "I—have sometimes—wondered—if—He wasn't!"

"Ah!" said Mary looking at him piercingly, "and yet they said that you believed on Him! Well, listen, now, you traitor! You have said that I was the only one who knew the truth about His heavenly origin. Yes, that is true. It was to me the angel came and told me what high honor Heaven was sending to me, a humble maiden. I have kept all His words in my heart. It is I who know how the power of the Most High came upon me. It is I who have pondered these great things all His wonderful life, and watched to see my Jesus grow up for His great mission. Yes, I know!

And *never* will I soil my Holy One by denying the truth about Him! God knows that I would give this heart of mine and let it be torn asunder and laid bare to the world to set Him free from His enemies. But never will I dishonor my God by telling cheap lies to save my Son for any man-planned kingdom. If God wills that He should go to His death that He may fulfill His plan for Him, so be it, but I will never deny the truth! Go, Judas, self-steeped soul, enemy of Jesus the Son of God! Traitor! *Satan!* Thinking to outwit God! *Go!* No word of mine shall ever deny the holy power of the Most High, nor thus undo the mischief that your traitor kiss has wrought!"

Mary turned her back upon him and walked from the room, closing the door with finality. Judas, darkly frowning, baffled, slid from the door and was gone into the night; and the morning of that saddest day of all the world crept softly into the sky, like one who knew its brightness was soon to be darkened by the sin of the world.

Then Salome crept softly to the door of her guest's room and quietly knelt beside her as she wept upon her bed.

"Mary, dear," she whispered with a sympathetic arm about her friend, "I couldn't help hearing what he said. Of course I feel the same way you do about Judas. I never did like him. And I can understand that you were angry;

but—wasn't there reason this time in what he said? It is true, isn't it, that the charge they have made against Him is that He claims to be the King of the Jews, the long expected Messiah, the Holy One that is to come, born miraculously? And wasn't Judas right in saying that if that could be denied, He might be set free? Mary, at a time of stress like this, and for so good a cause, surely there would be no harm in your saying that it is not true—that Joseph—or somebody else—*was* His father. What harm could there be in that? Why won't you do it, dear?"

"Because it is not *true!*" said Mary lifting her tear-stained face to look earnestly at her friend in the dim light of the dawn. "Because it is according to the angel's message, and God's word, that He was of heavenly origin. Because I *know* what I know! I would be most unworthy of my wonderful Son if I were to deny His heavenly Fatherhood."

"But Mary, not to *save* His life?"

"Not to save His life, Salome! He would not want it, my friend. You do not know Him if you think He would."

Then suddenly upon the outer door came insistent knocking and a sound of voices talking.

Hastily Salome rose and went to answer the knock.

"It is your other sons, Mary!" she whispered, coming

back. "They want to see you at once. Don't look so frightened, dear; nothing has happened. The Sanhedrin has not yet come together."

Then Mary went again to the outer room and stood among her stalwart sons.

"Mother, we have come to see you about Jesus," spoke the eldest of them. "He has got Himself into real trouble at last, just as we told you He would if a stop wasn't put to His nonsense. He is to be tried quite early this morning, in an hour perhaps, and according to all we can find out about it, the odds are entirely against Him. The Sanhedrin is disgusted with all the excitement and wild talk of miracles. That business about Lazarus being raised from the dead has put the finishing touch to it. And now there is no hope for Him, unless—well, Mother, we've thought of a way. At least a way has been suggested."

She gave him a quick bright look, with hope dawning in her eyes. Was there a way to save Him? Yet these brothers of His were not in sympathy with Him, she remembered with a sharp pang. Would it be a *possible* way? They had always disparaged His ministry, disagreed with His way of life, and called it visionary. They had driven Him from His home.

Then out spoke the youngest brother eagerly. He had

never been quite so hard as the rest, had always tried to smooth the way between them all, to placate and explain.

"Mother, don't look so worried. It's practically an easy thing to get Him off if you will only agree. Just a few words from you, and everything will be all right. I know it may be a bit embarrassing to you, but you won't mind, I'm sure, if this thing can only be hushed up and Jesus set free. Our family has never been mixed up in publicity this way, and we don't want to begin now. It's nothing much, Mother, it's just that claim that He is virgin born that is making all the trouble. If you will only be willing to say it wasn't so—it could be done in a few words and quite quietly, to a few who have influence—it could all be hushed up and Jesus released. Everyone would understand and respect you, Mother. All you would need to do would be to tell them that our father was of course Jesus' father too. And I'm sure that Father, if he were here, would quite approve. He was always so reasonable, and always treated Jesus just like one of us. Come, Mother, get your things on. There isn't much time to spare!"

Suddenly Mary clasped her hands and looked up, drawing a deep breath.

"Oh, if my Joseph were only here!" she cried. "He knew all about it. He would understand. God spoke to him in a

dream and told him that my Jesus was from on high, and
Joseph believed it. Oh, your father would understand, my
son, yes he would understand, and he and I could never
deny what God has done. My Jesus *is* the *very Son of God!*"

Out into the morning at last went the stalwart sons,
unable to move their frail little mother, marvelling at her
strength, and stubbornness, as they called it, over such a
small matter that meant so much to the family pride just
now. They walked along the waking streets where smug
Sanhedrin members took an eager way to Pilate's Hall,
rubbing their hands in satisfaction as they met one another
with gravely congratulatory bows. The prey was in their
hands at last. The troublesome One would soon be dealt
with, and the people return to reasonableness and ritual
and formality.

And Mary, as she waited for her friend to make ready,
knelt alone beside the bed whereon she had not slept that
night, and let her heart stand still before her God, yield-
ing her will to His, feeling the consciousness that He was
still using her, going over in her heart all the words of the
angel Gabriel. Ah! It did not look this morning as if all
nations could call her blessed, as the world counts blessed-
ness! Mother of a Son about to be tried for His life!

And a word from her, a little *lie*, could set Him free!

And perhaps undo the plan of the eternal God for the ages to come! But the God of gods had promised! He knew the end from the beginning! There was nothing to do but trust Him! In her sorrowing soul she bowed and said softly to Him once more:

"Behold the handmaid of the Lord; be it unto me according to Thy word," and she knew within herself that her precious privilege of suffering for her wonderful Son was not yet over.

Then she remembered the words of her cousin Elizabeth, long ago, especially those last few words: "Blessed is she that believed: for there shall be a performance of those things which were told her of the Lord."

And God had performed it all as He had told her, could she not trust the future of that Son with Him who had sent Him, as well as she had trusted His past?

Then suddenly with a stab of pain came the memory of old Simeon's words to her: "Yea, a sword shall pierce through thy own soul also." Was this what those words had meant? Her soul shrank within her in apprehension. And yet there was nothing she could do but trust, and if God could work His will through a crucified Jesus, who was she to try to prevent it by denying the great miraculous truth, and setting a lie ringing down the ages?

So Mary arose and went forth to Calvary.

Now on the way they passed the praetorium. A great crowd was assembled there, and as Mary and Salome skirted about it, they saw Mary's other sons.

The youngest one came and took her arm.

"What is it all about?" she asked fearfully as the crowd jostled her back against the wall.

Her son drew her up into a doorway where she could see over the heads of the people, and as they looked, there on the great stone platform of the place called The Pavement, came forth Pilate, and One after him clad in a purple robe with a crown of cruel thorns upon His head.

"There! You see, Mother," whispered her son, "they are mocking Him. That is my brother! Think of it, *my brother,* up before the eyes of the common herd! And *you* might have saved us all this by just a few words. But list! Pilate is speaking now. Hark, I want to hear what he says!"

Pilate's voice was clear, and the mob was suddenly hushed as he spoke. Mary heard the words quite distinctly:

"I bring Him forth to you, that ye may know that I find no fault in Him! Behold, the man!"

Mary caught her breath, and a great wave of hope rushed over her. If Pilate found no fault, why, surely He might be saved!

But suddenly from all about her there arose a cruel snarl of cries: "Crucify Him! Crucify Him!" Some of those voices, too, came from chief priests and officers. But Pilate's voice was ringing out again:

"Take *ye* Him and crucify Him: for *I* find no fault in Him."

Then up rose a cruel-faced man, wearing pompous robes, and claimed attention, speaking to Pilate, and hushing the mob into silence.

"We have a law," he said ominously, "and by our law He ought to die, because He made Himself *the Son of God!*"

Mary drew in her breath sharply.

"There it is, Mother, just as we told you!" her son whispered in her ear. "It is for that absurd claim they are killing Him, nothing else. And one word from you would set it all right. Do it now, Mother, while there is yet time! Do it now, and let us slip Him away out of sight quickly before the mob is roused again. I'll lead you up to Pilate. See, there is a way behind that group of men! Pilate does not want to crucify Him. He will listen to you if you will go."

But Mary's eyes were on her Son, that precious heavenly face with a glory in the eyes that other faces seemed not

to know. Those cruel thorns pressed into His loved brow,
that brow she had kissed and fondled when He was a little
babe! How her heart was wrung to see Him so, mocked
at and scorned, the great men of the council wishing to kill
Him! Her Holy One! That purple robe! With what dignity
He wore it! And even a thorny crown, how royally it sat
upon His brow! Why could they not see it, those chief
priests and scribes who called themselves wise; why could
they not realize with what royal bearing He wore the
robes put upon Him in scorn?

Ah! She could not stand it to see Him so! Almost she
yielded to her son's urgency. Almost! But then Pilate spoke
again. He was not speaking to the crowd now. He was
looking straight at Jesus. But she could hear every word.

"Whence art thou?"

Mary looked eagerly toward her Son. Now she would
have the word from His own lips. But no! He was not
speaking at all! What could it mean?

"There! Mother!" sneered the younger brother with con-
tempt in his voice. "There's your miracle-worker! He
hasn't the nerve to answer! He can't stand up for Himself!
My brother!"

But Pilate was speaking again:

"Speakest thou not unto me? Knowest thou not that I have power to crucify thee, and have power to release thee?"

Ah! Now He was answering at last.

"Thou couldst have no power at all against Me except it were given thee from above."

Mary drew back and pulled away from the urgency of the young arm that would have drawn her toward the stone seat of judgment where Pilate sat. No, that was her answer. It was not for her to deny God's wonders. "Thou couldst have no power at all against Me except it were given thee from above." That was her reminder that she was the handmaid of the Lord, that somehow this thing was of Him.

And then the crowd surged in. They were leading Him away. Her Jesus! Her precious baby!

She thought of Him in the manger smiling so sweetly from the straw. She remembered the wonderful star that had blazed forth over the stable where he lay. She thought of the shepherds who came to worship and their tale of angel-messages: Peace on earth! And He was being led away to be crucified! She thought of the wise men and their strange symbolic presents! She remembered prophecies about Him which she had not understood!

And now they were making Him bear His cross!

She caught one glimpse of Him through her tears as He sank under it. She remembered the promise of the angel that He was to be great and that God was to give Him the throne of his father David! And now He was lying on the pavement beneath a cross, a crown of thorns upon His head! The Son of God! She was not hearing her other son's words as he tried to lead her home away from it all, telling her that it was too late now. But though the words came with a thud against her soul she knew that even if it had not been too late she could not have denied His heavenly origin.

Calvary at last, and the awful sound of the hammers driving nails! Nails through the precious hands! Oh those rosy baby hands! She had so often laid reverent lips to kiss their palms! She sank with the other women on a hillock and covered her face, hearing those awful hammer blows! Her Jesus! Her precious Jesus! *Her Lord!*

Oh, could mortal mother bear those sounds and not cry out, *even a lie* to save Him? She rose and staggered up the hill. Her Babe of Bethlehem! Her sweet little Babe with His heavenly smile! Oh, if she might but just have permission from God to deny His origin and save Him yet!

She saw the insults that followed, she saw them spit into His precious face, and jeer. She saw them slap Him in the face with the backs of their gnarled hands, she saw them bartering His garments that she had wrought with such loving care. She heard them call upon Him to save Himself, to show His kingship!

She saw the blood drops falling down His brow from the cruel thorns! Oh could mortal mother endure that sight and not do something? *Anything!* Perhaps it was not too late even yet! Perhaps Pilate was up there near the cross and she could go and tell him that it was all an awful mistake!

But it was not a mistake! And she knew in her heart that even though she should lie to shield Him, He would claim His heavenly origin to the end! He *wanted* her to do the same.

She staggered to her feet and went nearer, dropping down at the very foot of the cross looking up, and He looked down and caught her glance! Through all His anguish, He yet had thoughts for her, and wanted her to understand that *He* knew what she was passing through, and that He was pleased, satisfied with her loyalty.

And then He spoke! Oh, wonder of wonders! He called John and gave her into his care! Ah! How precious! The tears flowed down without their former bitterness!

"But O, God in heaven! Will You let Your Son die with-

out a sign? Though You carry out Your purpose for the
ages through a crucified Jesus, will You not at least give
some sign to the world that He is the Son of God?"

Suddenly Mary realized that though it was high noon
darkness was coming down over the earth! Heaven itself
was putting out its light to condemn the awful deed, and
testify to the truth of the claim of the Holy One!

It was then the earthquake came! Strange quiverings of
the ground, awful rending of rocks, and rumblings! Ah,
God was showing the earth its awful sin!

Suddenly, beside her some one spoke. It was a voice she
did not know, perhaps a centurion standing by the cross,
but the words were spoken with profound earnestness and
conviction:

"Truly, this was the Son of God!"

Mary heard, and lifted her bowed head. Oh! Suppose she
had told a lie to save *Him*? She was glad, *glad* that she
had remained firm to the end. This one man at least had
been convinced of the truth even through her son's death,
and there would be others! She lifted trusting eyes to
heaven.

Then down at her feet, the lie, which had lain coiled like
a serpent, looking at her with great evil green eyes, ready
for her use should she weaken, slowly uncoiled and slunk

away—not to die, only to lie coiled and hidden, awaiting other times, when other souls less faithful through other years, should find it and bring it forth, to dishonor the eternal Son of God with blasphemies, and to deceive "them that perish; because they received not the *love of the truth* that they might be saved. . . . God shall send them strong delusion that they should believe a lie! that they all might be damned who believed not the truth but had pleasure in unrighteousness."